To Joan
1999/2000

Pop

KU-617-042

First published in Great Britain in 1996 by

BROCKHAMPTON PRESS,

20 Bloomsbury Street,

London WC1B 3QA.

a member of the Hodder Headline Group,

This series of little gift books was made by Frances Banfield, Andrea P.A. Belloli, Polly Boyd, Kate Brown, Stefano Carantini, Laurel Clark, Penny Clarke, Clive Collins, Jack Cooper, Melanie Cumming, Nick Diggory, John Dunne, Deborah Gill, David Goodman, Paul Gregory, Douglas Hall, Lucinda Hawksley, Maureen Hill, Dennis Hovell, Dicky Howett, Nick Hutchison, Douglas Ingram, Helen Johnson, C.M. Lee, Simon London, Irene Lyford, John Maxwell, Patrick McCreeth, Morse Modaberi, Tara Neill, Sonya Newland, Anne Newman, Grant Oliver, Ian Powling, Terry Price, Michelle Rogers, Mike Seabrook, Nigel Soper, Karen Sullivan and Nick Wells.

Compilation and selection copyright © 1996 Brockhampton Press.

All rights reserved. No part of this publication may be reproduced, stored in a retrieval system, or transmitted in any form or by any means, without the prior written permission of the copyright holder.

ISBN 1 86019 4346

A copy of the CIP data is available from the British Library upon request.

Produced for Brockhampton Press by Flame Tree Publishing, a part of The Foundry Creative Media Company Limited, The Long House, Antrobus Road, Chiswick W4 5HY.

Printed and bound in Italy by L.E.G.O. Spa.

THE LITTLE BOOK
OF
Flowers

Selected by Karen Sullivan

BROCKHAMPTON PRESS

Here's fine rosemary, sage, and thyme,
Come buy my ground ivy.
Here's fetherfew, gilliflowers and rue.
Come buy my knotted marjorum, ho!

Anonymous, *The Cries of London*

Keep not your roses for my dead, cold brow
The way is lonely, let me feel them now.

Arabella Smith

The walls, old and weather-stained, covered with
hollyhocks, roses, honey-suckles, and a great
apricot-tree; the casements full of geraniums...

Mary Russell Mitford, *Our Village*

Flowers have spoken to me more than I can tell in
written words. They are the hieroglyphics of angels,
loved by all men for the beauty of the
character, though few can decipher even
fragments of their meaning.

Lydia M. Child

Now folds the lily all her sweetness up,
And slips into the bosom of the lake:
So fold thyself, my dearest, thou, and slip
Into my bosom and be lost in me.

Alfred, Lord Tennyson

I'd choose to be a daisy,
If I might be a flower;
Closing my petals softly
At twilight's quiet hour;
And waking in the morning,
When falls the early dew,
To welcome Heaven's bright sunshine,
And Heaven's bright tear-drops, too.

Anonymous, 'I'd Choose to be a Daisy'

One of the most attractive things about the flowers is
their beautiful reserve.

Henry David Thoreau

Sweet Flower! that peeping from thy russet stem
Unfoldest timidly (for in strange sort
This dark, freize-coated, hoarse,
teeth-chattering Month
Hath borrowed Zephyr's voice,
and gazed upon thee
With blue voluptuous eye) alas,
poor Flower!

Samuel Taylor Coleridge

Pale primroses,
That die unmarried ere they can behold
Bright Phoebus in his strength.

William Shakespeare, *The Winter's Tale*

The little garden beyond is full of common flowers,
tulips, pinks, larkspurs, peonies, stocks, and carnations,
with an arbour of privet.

Mary Russell Mitford, *Our Village*

Man
You beheld the saddest and dreariest
of all the flowers of the earth
And as with other flowers you gave it a name
You called it Thought.

Jacques Prévert

God Almighty first planted a garden.
And indeed, it is the purest of human pleasures.

Francis Bacon

A thing of beauty is a joy forever:
Its loveliness increases; it will never
Pass into nothingness; but still will keep
A bower quiet for us, and a sleep
Full of sweet dreams, and health, and quiet breathing.
Therefore, on every morrow, are we wreathing
A flowery bank to bind us to the earth.

John Keats, 'Endymion'

The periwinkles, with their starry blue flowers,
and their shining myrtle-like leaves,
garlanding the bushes; woodbines and elder-trees
pushing out their small swelling buds...

Mary Russell Mitford, *Our Village*

Ophelia: There's rosemary, that's for remembrance;
pray you, love, remember. And there is pansies,
that's for thoughts.

William Shakespeare, *Hamlet*

Never was a spot more variously flowery: primroses
yellow, lilac white, violets of either hue, cowslips, oslips,
arums, orchises, wild hyacinths, ground ivy, pansies,
strawberries, heart's-ease, formed a small part of the
Flora of that wild hedgerow.

Mary Russell Mitford, *Our Village*

The foxglove bells, with lolling tongue,
Will not reveal what peals were rung
In Faery, in Faery,
A thousand ages gone.
All the golden claspers rang;
Only from the mottled throat
Never any echoes float.
Quite forgotten, in the wood,
Pale, crowded steeples rise...

Mary Webb

Daffydowndil to town
In a yellow petticoat and a green gown.

Traditional

That which above all yields
the sweetest smell in the air
is the violet.

Sir Francis Bacon

Buttercups and daisies,
Oh, the pretty flowers;
Coming ere the Spring-time,
To tell of sunny hours.

Mary Witt

Spring has come when you put
your foot on three daisies.

Proverb

And in the warm hedge grew
lush eglantine,
Green cow-bind and the
moonlight-coloured may.

Percy Bysshe Shelley

What's in a name? That which we call a rose,
by any other name would smell as sweet.

William Shakespeare, *Romeo and Juliet*

Here are sweet peas, on tiptoe for a flight
With wings of gentle flush o'er delicate white.

John Keats

A young soldier with his regiment in the First World
War took over a trench position from a Scottish
regiment. He wrote to *The Times* in 1917 to say that
'Standing on an oak table in the middle of the dug-out
was a shell-case filled with flowers, Madonna lilies,
mignonette, and roses.'

Thou art the Irish, fair among the fairest,
Who, armed with the golden rod
And winged with the celestial azure, bearest
The message of some God.

Henry Wadsworth Longfellow, 'Message'

A garden saw I full of blosmy boughs
Upon a river, in a grene mead,
There as sweetness evermore enow is,
With flowers e, blue, yellow, and red.

Geoffrey Chaucer, 'The Parlement of Foules'

The world's a garden; pleasures are the flowers,
Of fairest hues, in form and number many:
The lily, first, pure-whitest flower of any,
Rose sweetest rare, with pinked gilliflowers,
The violet, and double marigold,
And pansy too: but after all mischances,
Death's winter comes and kills with sudden cold
Rose, lily, violet, marigold, pink, pansies.

William Shakespeare, 'The Garden'

The pink, the primrose, cowslip, and daffodilly,
The hare-bell blue, the crimson columbine,
Sage, lettuce, parsley, and the milk-white lily,
The rose, and speckled flower called sops-in-wine;
Fine pretty king-cups, and the yellow boots
That grows by rivers, allow brooks.

Richard Barnfield, 'The Affectionate Shepherd'

O graceful Raphael, dare to vie
With the rich tints that paint the breathing mead?
The thousand-coloured tulip, violet's bell
Snow-clad and meek, the vermil-tinctured rose,
And golden crocus?

Joseph Warton, 'The Enthusiast'

First and best I love violets, and primroses, and
cowslips, and wood anemones, and the whole train of
field flowers; then roses of every kind and colour,
especially the great cabbage rose; then the blossoms of
the lilac and laburnum, the horse-chestnut, easters, the
jasmine, and the honeysuckle, and to close the list,
lilies of the valley, sweet peas, and the red pinks which
are found in cottagers' gardens.

Mary Russell Mitford, Letter to Sir William Elford, 1812

The fairest flowers of the season
Are our carnations...

William Shakespeare, *The Winter's Tale*

Roses in heaps were there, both red and white,
Lilies angelical, and gorgeous glooms
Of wall-flowers, and blue hyacinths, and blooms
Hanging thick clusters from light boughs...

Leigh Hunt, 'The Story of Rimini'

The snowdrop, and then the violet,
Arose from the ground with warm rain wet,
And their breath was mixed with fresh odour, sent
From the turf, like the voice and the instrument.

Percy Bysshe Shelley, 'The Sensitive Plant'

And the jessamine faint, and the sweet tuberose,
The sweetest flower for scent that blows;
And all rare blossoms from every clime
Grew in that garden in perfect prime.

Percy Bysshe Shelley, 'The Sensitive Plant'

The red rose cries, 'She is near, she is near;'
And the white rose weeps, 'She is late;'
The larkspur listens, 'I hear, I hear;'
And the lily whispers, 'I wait.'

Alfred, Lord Tennyson, 'Maud'

And the stately lilies stand
Fair in silvery light
Like saintly vestals, pale in prayer;
Their pure breath sanctifies the air,
And its fragrance fills the night.

Anonymous

The kiss of the sun for pardon,
The song of the birds for mirth,
One is nearer God's Heart in a garden
Than anywhere else on earth.

Dorothy Frances Gurney

There is a garden where lilies
And roses are side by side;
And all day between them in silence
The silken butterflies glide.

Francis Turner Palgrave, 'Eutopia'

Stately stand the sunflowers,
glowing down the garden-side,
Ranged in royal rank a row along
the warm grey wall,
Whence their deep disks
burn at rich midnoon afire with pride...
Here the full clove pinks and wallflowers
crown the love they claim.

Charles Algernon Swinburne, 'The Mill Garden'

When daisies pied and violets blue
And ladysmocks all silver-white
And cuckoobuds of yellow hue
Do paint the meadows with delight...

William Shakespeare, *Love's Labours Lost*

I wandered lonely as a cloud
That floats on high o'er vales and hills,
When all at once I saw a crowd,
A host, of golden daffodils;
Beside the lake, beneath the trees,
Fluttering and dancing in the breeze.

William Wordsworth, 'Daffodils'

To thinke God that after his image
You made, and thinketh all n'is but a fair
This world, and passeth soon as flowers fair.

Geoffrey Chaucer, 'Love Unfeigned'

Ennewed your colour
Is like the daisy flower
After the April shower.

John Skelton, 'To Mistress Isabel Pennell'

As Merry Margaret, this Midsummer flower.

John Skelton, 'To Mistress Margaret Hussey'

Strowe the ground with Daffadowndillies
And Cowslips, and King Cups, and loved Lillies.

Edmund Spenser, 'The Lay to Eliza'

Go, lovely Rose —
Tell her that wastes her time and me,
That now she knows,
When I resemble her to thee,
How sweet and fair she seems to be.

Edmund Waller, 'Go, Lovely Rose'

For a wild nosegay you will find the white water-lily
surrounded by the purple willow-herb,
the yellow loose-strife, the deep rose-colour of the
ragged robin and the exquisite blue
of the forget-me-not very imposing.

Mary Russell Mitford, Letter to John Ruskin, 1854

Flowers have time before they come to seed,
And she is young, and now must sport the while.

Samuel Daniel, 'Sonnet'

Lilies will languish; violets look ill,
Sickly the primrose; pale the daffodil;
The gallant tulip will hang down his head,
Like a virgin newly ravished;
Pansies will weep, and marigolds will wither,
And keep a fast and funeral together;
If Sappho droop, daisies will open never,
But bid goodnight, and close their lids forever.

Robert Herrick, 'The Sadness of Things for Sappho's Sickness'

Sweet rose, whose hue angrie and brave
Bids the rash gazer wipe his eye.

George Herbert, 'Vertue'

I would I had some flowers
o' th' spring that might
Become your time of day.

William Shakespeare, *The Winter's Tale*

One soft flame upturning
Seems, to his discerning,
Crocus in the shade.

Ebeneezer Jones, 'When the World Is Burning'

Beauty is but a flower
Which wrinkles will devour.

Thomas Nashe, 'In Time of Pestilence'

And I will make thee a bed of roses
With a thousand fragrant posies,
A cap of flowers, and a kirtle
Embroidered all with leaves of myrtle.

Christopher Marlowe, 'The Passionate Shepherd to His Love'

Go down to Kew in lilac time (it isn't far from London)
And you shall wander hand in hand
with love in Summer's wonderland.

Alfred Noyes, 'The Barrel Organ'

Thy gowns, thy shoes, thy beds of roses,
Thy cap, thy kirtle, and the posies
Soon break, soon wither, soon forgotten,
In folly ripe, in reason rotten.

Sir Walter Raleigh, 'The Nymph's Reply to the Shepherd'

Gather the rose of love, whilest yet is time.

Edmund Spenser, 'The Fairie Queene'

Yet marked I where the bolt of Cupid fell.
It fell upon a little western flower,
Before milk-white, now purple with love's wound,
And maidens call it love-in-idleness.

William Shakespeare, *A Midsummer Night's Dream*

'Tis the last rose of Summer,
Left blooming alone;
All her lovely companions
Are faded and gone.

Thomas Moore, 'The Last Rose'

I know a bank where the wild thyme blows,
Where oxlips and the nodding violet grows,
Quite overcanopied with luscious woodbines,
With sweet musk roses and with eglantine.

William Shakespeare, *A Midsummer Night's Dream*

Full many a flower is born to blush unseen,
And waste its sweetness on the desert air.

Thomas Gray, 'Elegy Written in a Country Churchyard'

If I should die, think only this of me:
That there's some corner of a foreign field
That is forever England. There shall be
In that rich earth a richer dust concealed;
A dust whom England bore, shaped, made aware,
Gave, once, her flowers to love, her ways to roam,
A body of England's, breathing English air,
Washed by the rivers, blest by suns of home.

Rupert Brooke, 'The Soldier'

My luve is like a red, red rose.

Robert Burns

With honeysuckle, over-sweet, festooned;
With bitter ivy bound;
Terraced with funguses unsound;
Deformed with many a boss
And closed scar, o'ercushioned deep with moss;
Bunched all about with pagan mistletoe;
And thick with nests of the hoarse bird
That talks, but understands not his own word;
Stands, and so stood a thousand years ago,
A single tree.

Coventry Patmore

Daffodils,
That come before the swallow dares, and take
The winds of March with beauty.

William Shakespeare, *The Winter's Tale*

To me the meanest flower that blows can give
Thoughts that do often lie too deep for tears.

William Wordsworth

Flowers...are a proud assertion that a ray of beauty
outvalues all the utilities of the world.

Ralph Waldo Emerson

The foxglove bells, with lolling tongue,
Will not reveal what peals were rung
In Faery, in Faery,
A thousand ages gone.
All the golden clappers hang
As if but now the changes rang;
Only from the mottled throat
Never any echoes float.
Quite forgotten, in the wood,
Pale, crowded steeples rise.

Mary Webb

Violets dim,
But sweeter than the lids of Juno's eyes.

William Shakespeare, *The Winter's Tale*

I like not lady-slippers,
Nor yet the sweet-pea blossoms,
Nor yet the flaky roses,
Red, or white as snow;
I like the chaliced lilies,
The heavy Eastern lilies,
The gorgeous tiger-lilies,
That in our garden grow!

Thomas Bailey Aldrich, 'Tiger-Lilies'

Rhadora! if the sages ask thee why
This charm is wasted on the earth and sky,
Tell them, dear, that if eyes were made for seeing,
Then Beauty is its own excuse for being:
Why thou wert there, O rival of the rose!
I never thought to ask, I never knew:
But in my simple ignorance, suppose
The self-same Power that brought me there
brought you.

Ralph Waldo Emerson, 'The Rhodora'

A Daisy and a Buttercup
Agreed to have a race,
A Squirrel was to be the judge
A mile off from the place.

The Squirrel waited patiently
Until the day was done –
Perhaps he is there waiting still,
You see – they couldn't run.

Mrs Molesworth, 'A Race'

Wee, modest, crimson-tipped flow'r,
Thou's met me in an evil hour;
For I maun crush among the stoure
Thy slender stem:
To spare thee now is past my pow'r
Thou bonie gem.

Robert Burns, 'To a Mountain Daisy'

I have sown upon the fields
Eyebright and Pimpernel
And Pansy and Poppy-seed
Ripen'd and scatter'd well,

And silver Lady-smock
The meads with light to fill
Cowslip and Buttercup,
Daisy and Daffodil;

King-cup and Fleur-de-lys
Upon the marsh to meet
With Comfrey, Watermint,
Loose-strife and Meadowsweet;

And all along the stream
My care hath not forgot
Crowsfoot's white galaxy
And love's Forget-me-not:

And where high grasses wave
Shall great Moon-daisies blink,
With Rattle and Sorrel sharp
And Robin's ragged pink.

Thick on the woodland floor
Gay company shall be,
Primrose and Hyacinth
And frail Anemone.

Perennial Strawberry-bloom
Woodsorrel's pencilled veil
Dishevel'd Willow-weed
And Orchis purple pale.

Robert Bridges, 'The Idle Flowers'

Wi' lightsome heart I pu'd a rose
Frae aff its thorny tree,
And my fause luver staw my rose,
But left the thorn wi' me.

Robert Burns, 'Ye Flowery Banks'

Through primrose tufts, in that green bower,
The periwinkle trailed its wreaths;
And 'tis my faith that every flower
Enjoys the air it breathes...

William Wordsworth, 'Lines Written in Early Spring'

And still she slept an azure-lidded sleep,
In blanched linen, smooth, and lavender'd...

John Keats, 'The Eve of St Agnes'

Fair daffodils we weep to see you
haste away so soon
As yet the early rising sun
has not attained his noon
Stay, stay until the hasting day has run
But to the ev'en song
And having prayed together
we will go with you along.

George Herbert, 'Fair Daffodils'

White hawthorn, and the pastoral eglantine;
Fast fading violets cover'd up in leaves;
And mid-May's eldest child,
The coming musk-rose, full of dewy wine,
The murmurous haunt of flies on summer eves.

John Keats, 'Ode to a Nightingale'

How could such sweet and wholesome hours
Be reckoned but with herbs and flowers?

Andrew Marvel, 'The Garden'

I remember, I remember
The roses, red and white,
The violets, and the lily-cups –
Those flowers made of light!

Thomas Hood, 'I Remember, I Remember'

All the names I know from nurse:
Gardener's garters, Shepherd's purse,
Bachelor's buttons, Lady's smock,
And the Lady Hollyhock.

Robert Louis Stevenson, 'The Flowers'

April showers bring forth May flowers.

Proverb

Gather ye rosebuds while ye may,
Old Time is still a-flying:
And this same flower that smiles to-day
To-morrow will be dying.

Robert Herrick

Give fools their gold, and knaves their power;
Let fortune's bubbles rise and fall;
Who sows a field, or trains a flower,
Or plants a tree, is more than all.

John Greenleaf Whittier

Love's language may be talked with these;
To work out choicest sentences
No blossoms can be meeter;
And, such being used in Eastern blowers,
Young maids may wonder if the flowers
Or meanings could be sweeter.

Elizabeth Barrett Browning

I was born under a kind star
In a green world withouten any war;
My eyes opened on quiet fields and hills,
Orchards and gardens, cowslips, daffodils,
Love for my rising-up and lying-down,
Amid the beautiful pastures green and brown –
The rose leaned through my window set ajar –
I was born under a kind star.

Katherine Tynana, 'I was Born Under a Kind Star'

Meadows trim with daisies pied,
Shallow brooks and rivers wide.

John Milton, 'L'Allegro'

The lake looked to me, I knew not why, dull and melancholy, and the weltering on the shores seemed a heavy sound. I walked as long as I could amongst the stones of the shore. The wood rich in flowers; a beautiful yellow, palish flower, that looked thick, round, and double, and smelt very sweet – I supposed it was a ranunculus. Crowfoot, the grassy-leaved rabbit-toothed white flower, strawberries, geranium, scentless violets, anemones two kinds, orchids, primroses. The heckberry very beautiful, the crab coming out as a low shrub. Met a blind man, driving a very large beautiful Bull, and a cow – he walked with two sticks. Came home by Clappersgate. The valley very green; many sweet views up to Rydale head...

Dorothy Wordsworth, Journal entry, 14 May 1800

I sing of brooks, of blossoms,
birds and bowers,
Of April, May, of June and July-flowers.

Robert Herrick, 'The Argument of His Book'

These flowers, which were splendid and sprightly,
Waking in the dawn of the morning,
In the evening will be a pitiful frivolity,
Sleeping in the cold night's arms.

Pedro Calderón de la Barca

Land of kind dreams
where the mountains are blue,
Where brownies are friendly
and wishing comes true!
Through your green meadows
they dance hand in hand –
Little odd people
of Buttercup Land.

Beatrix Potter, *Buttercup Land*

Whether the flower looks better in the nosegay than in
the meadow where it grew and we had to wet our feet
to get it! Is the scholastic air any advantage?

Henry David Thoreau

Every flower is a soul blossoming in Nature.

Gérard de Nerval

NOTES ON ILLUSTRATIONS

Page 6 *Sunflowers* by Vincent Van Gogh (National Gallery, London). Courtesy of The Bridgeman Art Library; **Page 11** *Among the Flowers*. Courtesy of The Laurel Clark Collection; **Page 12** *The Garden Path* by Elizabeth Cameron Mawson (Cooper Fine Arts Ltd., London). Courtesy of The Bridgeman Art Library; **Page 15** *The Garden at Giverny* by Claude Monet (Christie's, London). Courtesy of The Bridgeman Art Library; **Page 17** *Alfalfa, St Deins 1885* by George Seurat (National Galleries of Scotland, Edinburgh). Courtesy of The Bridgeman Art Library; **Page 19** *Vase of Flowers, c.1881-82* by Claude Monet (Courtauld Institute Galleries, University of London). Courtesy of The Bridgeman Art Library; **Page 20** *Sunflowers in a Herbaceous Border* by George Samuel Elgood (Christopher Wood Gallery, London). Courtesy of The Bridgeman Art Library; **Page 22** *Assorted Flowers*. Courtesy of The Laurel Clark Collection; **Page 25** *Young Girl in the Iris Garden, Giverny* by Max Agostini (Galerie Martin-Caille Matignon, Paris). Courtesy of The Bridgeman Art Library; **Page 27** *The Grandfather* by Carl Larsson (Sundborn, Sweden). Courtesy of The Bridgeman Art Library; **Page 29** *The Rose Garden at Hayes Place, Kent* by Alice Orde (Christopher Wood Gallery, London). Courtesy of The Bridgeman Art Library; **Page 30** *Primroses, Violets and Other Flowers* by J. Worsley (Christopher Wood Gallery, London). Courtesy of The Bridgeman Art Library; **Page 32** *Flowers in a Vase* by Pierre Auguste Renoir (Private Collection). Courtesy of The Bridgeman Art Library; **Page 34** *Seven Flower Arrangements*. Courtesy of The Laurel Clark Collection; **Pages 36-7** *The Artist's Garden at Giverny* by Claude Monet (Musée d'Orsay, Paris). Courtesy of The Bridgeman Art Library; **Page 39** *Purple Poppies* by Claude Monet (Museum Boymans-Van Beuningen, Rotterdam). Courtesy of The Bridgeman Art Library; **Page 41** *Summer Flowers* by Helen Allingham (Christopher Wood Gallery, London). Courtesy of The Bridgeman Art Library; **Page 42** *White Lily Pads at Giverny* by Max Agostini (Galerie Martin-Caille Matignon, Paris). Courtesy of The Bridgeman Art Library; **Page 44** *Flower Arrangements with Ivy*. Courtesy of The Laurel Clark Collection; **Page 47** *Garden at Vetheuil* by Claude Monet (Christie's, London). Courtesy of The Bridgeman Art Library; **Page 50** *Dean Hole's Garden, Rochester* by Ernest Arthur Rowe (John Spink Fine Watercolours, London). Courtesy of The Bridgeman Art Library; **Page 53** *Vase of Lilac* by Mary Cassatt (Private Collection). Courtesy of The Bridgeman Art Library; **Page 54** *A Hillside Garden in Westmoreland* by John Arthur Black (John Noot Galleries, Broadway, Worcestershire). Courtesy of The Bridgeman Art Library; **Page 57** *Spring Flower Arrangements with Ribbon*. Courtesy of The Laurel Clark Collection; **Pages 58-9** *A Mediterranean Garden* by Tom Mostyn (Christie's, London). Courtesy of The Bridgeman Art Library.

Acknowledgements: The Publishers wish to thank everyone who gave permission to reproduce the quotes in this book. Every effort has been made to contact the copyright holders, but in the event that an oversight has occurred, the publishers would be delighted to rectify any omissions in future editions of this book. Alfred Noyes, from 'The Barrel-Organ', from Collected Poems, reprinted courtesy of John Murray (Publishers) Ltd; *Dorothy Wordsworth's Journals* reprinted courtesy of William Collins Sons & Co Ltd, 1987; © Robert Ditchfield Ltd, 1987; *Good News Study Bible*, published by Thomas Nelson, 1986, extracts reprinted with their kind permission; *Penguin Book of Japanese Verse*, translated by Geoffrey Bownas and Anthony Thwaite, published by Penguin 1964, and reprinted with their permission; Beatrix Potter reproduced courtesy of Frederick Warne & Co., a division of Penguin Books.